Inspira
and U

MW01229950

Image
Confidence
Esteem

Monique K. Turrentine

ISBN-13: 978-1973859468

ISBN-10: 1973859467

Studio Griffin
A Publishing Company
Garner, North Carolina
www.studiogriffin.net

Image Confidence Esteem
Inspirations to Enhance and Uplift Your Life

Cover Design by Ruth E. Griffin
Image by Sergey Nivens/Adobe Stock

Blog: http://imageconfidenceesteem.wordpress.com
Email: imageconfidenceesteem@gmail.com

Printed in U.S.A

Acknowledgement

I thank Jesus for fulfilling my dreams and purpose to inspire others. These original writings started as my prayers and answered prayers. My friends and church family have always been a source of inspiration and laughter. I am most grateful for my amazing family, whose love and prayers continue to help me experience life fully; for my sister's dedication, my brothers' strength, the life lessons from my father and mother- especially my mother's commitment to see this work manifest, and the peaceful outlook on life from my grandparents. I dedicate this book to my family, who have always been faithful supporters in my endeavors.

CONTENTS

Introduction

As we go through the journey of life, we don't always get "it" right, whatever "it" is- love, faith, relationships, jobs and living out our dreams. Each of us has a story that can influence and impact others. This is my story.

This book starts with a chapter on how to 'Enhance Your Life' because most of my writings, which began almost a decade ago, came at a time of self-discovery when I was discovering my own value and value to others. Recognizing that people are like translucent images, and although at times it may feel as though we're unnoticed, we're still able to allow light to shine through. So, life is the light that helps us understand who we are, and that our interactions with other people enhance our life. 'Continually believe that you are valued and valuable' has been the core purpose of Image Confidence Esteem (I.C.E.), an image consulting business that I founded almost twenty years ago.

While in college, I had changed my major almost every semester and started my junior year feeling lost and without a sense of purpose, suffered the loss of my grandmother who also was influential in my upbringing, and what felt like the loss of my parents (who were going through a separation at the time). I became depressed and took a leave from college. I found that I no longer enjoyed life. But God surrounded me with loving people, like my mom, sister and my best friend, at a time when I wanted to be alone. They encouraged me, lifted my spirits and made me laugh, even when I didn't want to smile. Through that, God increased my faith, He showed me the creativity that He gave me; He helped me to discover my purpose and His plans for my life. I started designing clothes, which were later showcased in two spring fashion shows on campus when I returned to college. As I was designing, I heard God say, "image, confidence, esteem". It was through the image and confidence in Christ that boosted my self-esteem. I rediscovered a fulfilling life, graduated from college, and my parents reconciled their differences and renewed their vows. I remember praying to God that if He got me through that season, with His help I would encourage everyone I encountered.

But my story didn't stop there. It was just getting started. Chapter Two focuses on faith. Faith is the ability to believe in even the unimaginable. When your dream is revealed to you and you set your hopes on it, do you have the faith to believe in it? To see it come to fruition? The messages in this chapter will inspire you to believe again; while the next chapter, 'Positive Vision', guides you from growing your faith to implementing your dreams and passions with plans to excel in life. We then move through Chapter Four, which offers encouragement that faith allows you to confidently live out your dreams and the vision you have for your life.

I started I.C.E. because I've always had a passion for seeing the best in people and helping people to see the best in themselves. I was designing clothes and helping people wear their outfits in a way that expressed their best qualities. I was living out my dreams. And after ending an engagement in 2006, with faith, I decided to pursue a childhood dream to obtain my cosmetology license. Then I was laid off from my job during the mortgage crisis in 2008, so I became a full-time cosmetologist. During this time of conversation and interpersonal connection, I learned so much about my clients, and recognized that my God-given skills and abilities went beyond hairstyling or makeup artistry. Our conversations involved stories about love, relationships, faith and life. I became passionate about focusing on enhancing my clients' image, confidence and self-esteem. My clients would mention that they felt uplifted and inspired during our interactions. That's when God gave me the vision to write inspirational messages that would help all people recognize who they are as an individual, how to value their own and other's lives, and how to enhance their life.

Chapter Five helps us to understand that life is a process and nothing comes without proper planning and experiencing trials to take hold of the life you desire. Chapter Six is about love. Love is inevitable. You can't experience a full life without love. And as the book comes to an end, we connect to where we started, recognizing the importance of valuing yourself and others, on the topic about relationships. You must first love God, then yourself, before you can love others. When you learn and exemplify unconditional love, you're more successful in your relationships. The final chapter is about following the leader, ultimately Christ. You're not alone in the journey. God created you for the life you live today and the life you're capable of living tomorrow. Follow His plan to live life abundantly. And enjoy your life with encouragement along the way.

My goal is to inspire people to live authentically. After reading this book, my prayer is that you become more self-aware and confident, and grateful for your life every day. You may even find that you'll want to revisit sections of the book throughout your life journey; and I encourage you to do so.

Chapter 1
Enhance Your Life

Monique K. Turrentine

Enhance Your Life

If humans were viewed as fruit trees, would they merely be admired because of their fashion or their friends? An apple tree is not as pretty to look at if it has no apples, for then it would look like any other tree. It is because it is made to produce a healthy item for us, that it is appreciated and valued.

Appreciate and love your life, you are valuable!

Integrity

Have integrity about yourself and recognize your value. You're only as valuable as you see yourself and how you portray 'you' to others. Don't let rejection, denial or setbacks determine your outcome. When you're confident and act with integrity – that's when you're in control of what happens in and to your life.

Face It

When you honestly face and deal with the pain of your past, you're able to make better decisions moving forward. Each day and several moments therein each day, we're faced with making decisions - decisions that impact our health, sanity and well-being. Make honest decisions that accurately reflect the true you. Rediscover yourself in the process of getting to and through each day.

Desensitize Your Senses

Ever wonder why looking for something that stinks takes more of your time and energy than embracing the thing that smells good? People will turn over every trash can and throw away everything in the refrigerator to find and get rid of an awful scent. But when something smells good and is pleasing to your senses, you can barely sit back and enjoy the aroma.

Are you spending too much time seeking the stinking things in life? Regroup, refocus and desensitize your senses to the stinky things so that they do not monopolize your energy and you can spend more time recycling the freshness.

In the Sanctuary

Your body is a temple, so observe how you take care of it. Every part of your body serves a purpose. In your system, nothing is stagnant; everything is operative, rhythmic and reproductive. Your growth should not be stumped by failing to make necessary changes to live a healthy lifestyle. This is your chance at living in your full potential. Live well!

Get UP

Get clean, get dressed, gather your belongings and go!

It takes hope and belief to avoid pressing snooze at the start of your day. Believe in more than what you saw and experienced yesterday. Revive yourself and hope for the best. Yesterday didn't end without proper provision for today. Perform today; because today won't finish until it's qualified for tomorrow. Don't fear the unknown, but question the doubt and attain the unthinkable. Each day and every moment in the day is an opportunity to get up and get on with life.

Get in the Sun

There are life forms in all creation to remind us that we're not alone. We're here to engage and enjoy the beauty around us. It's amazing that even when we think we are alone, we'll see a bird fly by, hear a cricket chirp, smell a flower or taste fruit. Take advantage of the daylight and the times we have to live fully and enjoy God's blessings.

What are You Looking for God to Do?

Are you contemplating giving up because you may have missed His voice? Maybe you think it's "not my time" and you're looking for a sign.

Where did your plan end and His begin? Better yet, has your plan ended? Are you still enforcing your way?

At what point, do you live, "let go and let God"?

Who are you looking for? What are you waiting on? Do His plans now sound that unrealistic?

Chapter 2
Faith

Monique K. Turrentine

Faith

"...to put off your old self...to be made new in the attitude of your minds; and to put on the new self, created to be like God..." (Ephesians 4:22-23, NIV)

Daily, develop the type of faith that exceeds all expectations. The kind of faith that boosts your confidence and invigorates your soul.

Monique K. Turrentine

Make-Believe

I remember as a kid I enjoyed playing 'make-believe', believing love was easy to come by, and that the first man I met would be the man of my dreams. We would immediately fall in love, get married and live happily-ever-after. I would pretend that work was like having a picnic on a bright and sunny day with all my friends and family. Make-believe was my favorite pastime. Why has it changed? Why do I no longer 'make-believe'? Have the realities of life, trials with love and the continued journey to find fulfillment in my work led to disbelief? We often settle in our minds that we can't make-believe. However, I wonder, if we make our beliefs into reality, then we'll have the life we've dreamed of.

Get in the House

If you spent most of your childhood playing outdoors, then you probably remember your parent or loved one calling to you, "get in the house" before it got dark. It was a cherished sound, a reminder that someone was looking for you and awaiting your presence.

As adults, often we don't hear the phrase "get in the house". But if you stay out long enough, you'll hear a soft ringing or internal alarm calling "come into My house". If you've ever thought that no one cared to call you in, then think again.

God always has an open invitation and calls you to "come into His house". It's where you're safe, loved and fed good Word. If you're on the block and wondering which home He's calling you to, just stretch out your hand and pray - He'll guide you to the right place.

Keep Believing

There's a story written about a man who was very rich and lived life the right way. He had a wealthy and healthy family, mansions, animals and hired workers. Then one day his belief system was tested: people began to wonder if he was truly a good man; and, if he earned his wealth honestly. He started losing his wealth. The mansions were taken away, and his family members passed away. Then his health began to fail. Everyone speculated if he still believed in God. But, the man knew it was not easier to give up, though extremely anguished and frustrated. He kept trusting the One he believed in for all he had; and that his God would restore his health. It's never easier to "throw in the towel" just because you lost what you thought was your most valuable possession. The man didn't give up. He believed in God, and was later restored to excellent health, blessed with supportive friends and family, and became wealthier than ever before. Keep believing; it is never easier to give up!

Redirect Your Attention

Do you ever find yourself replaying in your mind the experiences of the day, comments people made, your responses and reactions, or things you witnessed? Only to have those same memories replay along with previous days' experiences and communications later? How is it that the things resting on our minds the longest are the things of least importance? Why do we place value on worthless items, while losing valuable time? Looking behind rather than focusing on the moment and day ahead? Today is the day to remember the best experience, a positive, impactful comment, learn from one mistake and learn to forgive yourself of everything else.

Go For It, or Let It Go!

Every decision in life is just that critical: to go for it or to let it go. You could either take advantage of the privileged life or take it for granted. You can decide to develop a program that will outlive your name or live out what people call you. What do you want to be known for? How will you leave your legacy? Making an important decision today, although it seems overwhelming, can make a difference for yours' and someone else's tomorrow. Go forward with the plan, and don't let it go!

So, What Have You Learned?

When seasons come to an end, reflect on the lessons learned, so that you don't have to repeat any mistakes. Remember a challenging moment so you won't be hindered from progressing next time. You've acquired peace by listening, love by caring and self-discipline by abstaining. What you learned is to exercise the knowledge you already have. Trust that no good deeds or works are without wisdom and direction. Your experiences in life are preceded and authored by the Creator of them all. You've learned to trust; now, live by faith!

It's Not My Condition

We believe God for everything else, but 'that'.

When you ask someone to pray for you, there's an inkling of belief that you may just need a little more encouragement for living in what you're in, and not living in the 'what's to come'. Am I to believe that where I am is it? No. I believe for where I am going. Am I to believe in the condition I'm in? No. I believe in who I am in Christ.

Your vision and dream aren't always realized by others.

After years of no manifestation in sight, others will try to get you to believe in your condition; to forfeit the promise and just deal with what's been the norm.

Yes, believe God for 'that', even when the odds are stacked against you, and when people think it's just not your time yet, set your sights on and belief in God!

Chapter 3
Positive Vision

Monique K. Turrentine

Positive Vision

Today, make a list of all the things you would like to experience over the next six to twelve months. After making the list, form an action plan on how to make it a reality. And most of all, have faith that God will bring it all to pass and that these wonderful experiences will truly happen! This is a start of a new way of thinking...a new vision for your new year!

Opportune Time

A "yes" preceded by prayer can be a future disaster. Learn to discern the right opportunities for you now and later. Build upon good decisions that will allow you to advance in life. Seek wisdom to understand where a decision will lead you and how it may affect others, especially those connected to you.

Heir-Line: Who's Washing Your Hair?

So, what's the importance of freeing your hair of debris? Is it true that if you don't frequently wash (shampoo) your hair, eventually the dirt will just fall off? No!

Frequent cleansing is vital to allowing the appropriate nutrients in. It is similar to when people allow others to speak negatively to them or when we speak negatively to someone. Ask yourself, who is drawing the line on what you allow to enter your mind. Don't hesitate to overcome a situation with a positive, encouraging statement. When your head is clogged with debris/negativity, wash it clean with positive affirmations.

What Do You Know?

I asked several people their opinion on the matter, and the response was the same… "idk".

I've finally learned shorthand, but it's inhibited my ability to properly communicate. My English syntax has been misconfigured and I'm no longer understood by others. So, what do you know? In an effort to conform to distorted simplicity, I've caused confusion.

Don't be confused; what you think and what you say is what it is.

Standardized Tests

Standardized tests, aren't those just for kids? Adults take standardized tests too. They happen when you're tested on your standards and whether or not you've established them. People shouldn't be able to take advantage of you, nor take you for granted. What standards have you set for yourself? Have you lived up to and expected others to respect them? The next time you take a standardized test, remember you're only tested on the information you've clearly defined.

Zero In

Zero is the only number and word that we've recognized to mean the absence of, or an utter failure. If we get a zero as a grade, it usually means that we put forth no effort. Even when the word zero is used with another word, like zero tolerance, it means to not tolerate at all. Surprisingly, the phrase "zero in on" doesn't mean the absence of, but it means to focus all your attention and to aim directly at something. Has your focus become a failure or has it been interrupted? Have you lost your direction on what you were aiming to achieve? Circle back to what you're most passionate about to 'zero in' on your ultimate plan.

Peace

As you enter a new season, consider where you are headed. Perhaps you're at a crossroad in your life and your next steps may not be clear. Well, there is hope! Whatever has brought you to this season, He will bring you through it.

So be at peace, even in times of uncertainty. A new season comes with a plan. Plan your day; plan for your life, or at least the next few years. Seasons are more peaceful when you can enjoy when they start, and when they end.

Look at All Things

In life, certain occurrences have the tendency to place your focus on the one thing going wrong – whether it's your job, health or a relationship. We put so much emphasis on that thing we despise, we don't allow our thoughts to consider all the other things. We get frustrated and cause our negative attitude to discount the many things that are going right. We forget that the one setback, although it may feel like several setbacks, is not representative of our full life. Consider the big picture, your whole outlook on life, and look at all things – it's better and more fulfilling than the one or few things you wish you could change right now.

Oh Taste & See

Get a taste of the real thing before reverting to the familiar. Familiarity may feel comforting – but is it healthy for you? Expecting and getting the real thing can bring about a new sense of direction.

O taste and see that the Lord is good! (Psalms 34:8, KJV)

Foresight

Imagine the tallest building or the longest bridge seen from many miles away. Even from the furthest or highest peak, in view of the bigger scheme of things, most large things or issues are myopic. This is like when we finally accomplish an intense project or task - the memory of the pre-conceived end is often vague.

Well, what is so unique about foresight? When we look at something from a different angle, we realize the things we highlighted or perceived as important, such as the large road blocks, measure out to be small stones.

The things we make a big deal of, though God says it's already handled, may take more time for us to recuperate from than reflecting on the real lesson.

Can You See It?

How do you help people see what you can't grasp? You describe it! Every elaborate detail should be explained to engulf the senses to the extent that it's overwhelming and breathtaking. Even when you can't take hold of it, you know it's present and you believe in what it is.

Can you discover the depths of God? Can you [by searching] discover the limits of the Almighty [ascend to His heights, extend to His widths, and comprehend His infinite perfection]? (Job 11:7, AMP)

So let us know and become personally acquainted with Him; let us press on to know and understand fully the [greatness of the] Lord [to honor, heed, and deeply cherish Him]. His appearing is prepared and is as certain as the dawn, and He will come to us [in salvation] like the [heavy] rain, like the spring rain watering the earth. (Hosea 6:3, AMP)

Watch This

Take a step back when you think you know exactly what God means when He reveals things to you. Let me explain, it's not easy to just figure out. You see, just because He shows you one thing and then it seems to align with another, you haven't quite figured it out. You don't know the end.

Allow God to show and tell.

Capture, but don't captivate. It's never a closed book. You can't pen or pin God.

He's just that amazing.

Just watch and see, and let Him do the rest.

(Inspired by Philippians 4:4-9, AMP)

Chapter 4
Confidence

Monique K. Turrentine

Confidence

This is a season of renewal. Put on Confidence! Confidence is about gratitude: be thankful for the skin you're in, your shape, your size, your hair and all your physical and spiritual attributes. How we portray our inner and outward appearances is a reflection of our gratitude to our Creator.

The exchange of a compliment (yes, it means giving and receiving compliments) is accepting and appreciating our image.

It first starts with wearing a smile, a real smile!

That's confidence – head up, chest out, big smile!

"You look great!"

Even when you don't feel you do, just say:

"Thank you! You too!"

Confidence in God

How would you describe your God? How would you explain your relationship with God? Who is He to you? Do you know Him better than you know your best friend or spouse?

In order to know who you are and what you are called to do/capable of doing, you must continue to get to know your Creator.

Spitting Image

We've been taught to believe that to look like the spitting image of someone else, means to look just like them. So, could you say that you look like the spitting image of your Father? We all have God (our Father) in us, so why don't we resemble Him? If we are to appear to be 'spit' from our Creator/Father, then people should see the mirror image of Him in us.

Let 'em Shine

The more successful you become, the more you have to be aware of your own insecurities. If gaining success means not being afraid or intimidated by your successors, then maintaining success means letting and helping those around you shine. Have you ever noticed that when one candle is lit, it's not as visible or bright as when there are other lit candles around it? So let 'em all shine!

Masquerade Ball

Dolled up, suit and tie, pumps and wing tips. This ball is sure to get newsworthy clips and buzz feeds. Many people are dying to be part of the "in" crowd.

We step out wearing shimmery masks so no one sees the social alienation, and now what's up is upside down. When you're not recognized in the 'mass-querade', look up – there's still One who knows you without the mask.

How Am I?

Usually we're so concerned with "who am I?" – that we lose sight of "how am I?" Whether the question relates to 'how am I <u>feeling</u>', or 'how am I <u>going to do this'</u>, or 'how am I <u>going to get through that'</u> – it's important to do an emotional, mental, physical and spiritual self-checkup, and frequently. An annual physical health exam with your physician isn't enough to monitor your overall well-being. You should feel most comfortable being transparent and honest with yourself. So, how am I?

Give Thanks

In 'The Magic' by Rhonda Byrne, she teaches us to give thanks for everything in our lives. As we give thanks for the various things in our lives, we invite more goodness in those areas. She says that giving thanks is truly the "magic" to having a good life. If you feel like you're lacking in a certain area (i.e. relationships, finances, career, and health) - start there and sincerely thank God for the little that you have in those areas. Let's witness together the "magic" that will return to us.

Converse

So, you think conversations are overrated? One minute you find yourself daydreaming while someone tells you about their day, and the next minute you find yourself conversing through text messages. What's all the waiting about if it's only to further converse?

It's just as easy to "say and respond" without criticism, judgment or fear. Is conversation a test of your confidence and faith?

Sometimes, half of what people talk about is just a façade, or an over-exaggerated story.

It's better to think than to hear yourself speak. Especially when you're not certain of what you're speaking about.

Just "listen and respond", and you'll communicate more effectively.

Chapter 5
Life is a Process

Monique K. Turrentine

I'm Capable of Doing This

Are you aware of your own capabilities? What about your inabilities? When seeking advancement in life, we're often questioned about what we're capable of doing. The truth is we're capable of doing a lot, even things we don't yet know. But our inabilities stack up as well. I once heard a pastor say, "You may not know what you're going to do, but at least know what you're not going to do." Give yourself some parameters, know what you're capable of doing and know what you're unwilling to sacrifice.

It is Here

What is it that you are looking for? Do you realize that it's already here? Whatever you are preparing for means you are that much closer to seeing it, having it and grabbing hold of it. Preparation also ensures that once you see it, you do not lose sight of it, do not stop planning for its growth, nor give up caring for it.

Move to the Next Page

In the last book you've read, did you find that it was hard to proceed to the next chapter? When reading a good novel, it's interesting how we can get so engaged in the plot and characters that we don't want to move on from the last exciting moment, especially if we're unsure of whether it will have a good ending. It can be easy to forget that we are also part of a story. And our story is destined to have a good ending.

Make right decisions in the twists and turns in life. Avoid the dog-ear pages, placing life on hold or prolonging the process by revisiting the past. It's good to acknowledge significant moments in life. The story is always better when you turn the page and get on with the next chapter…in your life.

This calls for a new chapter, a new start in the abundant life!

Influence

I was once focused on what I was doing and how it made me feel, rather than whom I was there to influence. I left one career feeling fully accomplished, to only enter another feeling hopeless. Thinking my responsibilities were too mundane to have any true meaning, I settled on the fact that I chose to be a vessel.

"Any way I could be used, use me Lord," is what I said, but quickly forgot my sacrifice and selfishly thought about my "feelings".

"This task is not making me feel anything, not fulfilled, not complete," I complained.

Then He reminded me, "you said use me!"

As the song resonates, "…use me Lord, to show someone the way and enable me to say, my storage is empty and I am available to you…my life I give to you, I do what you say do." Now the reason I work truly has meaning. So, I sit back free from the emotions and feelings, to be open to a greater cause, and I am grateful; this time life is not about me. Our life is about influence. It's time to Influence!

Let People See Me in My Process

I can barely recognize myself, so I'm sure they won't see me either.

But it's not about people seeing me. The purpose of going through the process is for people to see Christ in me. I shouldn't recognize myself because I'm becoming renewed through Him. Going through the process can be difficult when you're trying to become who you were. It's best when you're transparent and authentic about what it's really like to be tempted, fall and get back up to get it right.

(Inspired by 2 Corinthians 4:16, AMP)

Gain

You may now be at a point in your life where you feel you have gained wealth, an education, a successful career, and a healthy family. All you have gained though often becomes overwhelming to maintain, with more challenges and investments.

If what you have is the center of your complaints, then prioritize your goals, and establish a new way to move forward without being overtaken.

Gain new insight on the opportunities at hand and be willing to accept some and decline others.

Yank the Root

Getting out the root of a vegetable or plant is not easy; neither is getting to the root of an issue. I remember an age-old term "yank", which means to pull or remove abruptly and vigorously, and I think it is the best way to get a tough root. There are also times when potted plants become 'rootbound' (there is little soil, and water is no longer getting to the plant), similar to when the root of an issue has gotten so deep that you almost forgot what has caused your frustration. Then it's time to get the issue out of your head and in the open to discuss, like replanting the plant in a bigger pot. The process of replanting involves cutting the rotted parts and pruning other areas. When things in life lead to frustration, figuring out its cause may require "yanking the root", removing the rotted issues and letting growth take its proper course in a better suited environment.

"But blessed is the man who trusts me, GOD, the woman

who sticks with GOD. They're like trees replanted in Eden, putting down roots near the rivers—Never a worry through the hottest of summers, never dropping a leaf, Serene and calm through droughts, bearing fresh fruit every season." (Jeremiah 17:8, MSG)

You Gotta See My Scar!

When I was wounded, I didn't want anyone to know. I didn't want to interact with friends because I thought they would see my scar. But then I realized that I wasn't letting the healing take its course. Healing from wounds whether spiritual, emotional or physical are similar, in that exposure helps the healing take its proper course. When I allowed people to see my scar, it became a communal healing. They began sharing their hurt and were healed. They shared how they got through similar situations and it aided my healing process. I'm not afraid to let you see my scar and healing process.

Bob and Weave

It's a talent, and a skill to strategically move in and out of situations unscathed. But the emotions you don't deal with today will gravely impact you and others you encounter tomorrow. It's not a matter of "juking and jiving" or avoiding confrontations or even avoiding honest conversations. You need to bob and weave.

To bob and weave is to have the ability to successfully and strategically have the honest conversations to deal with the pain, hurt and offense, and for both parties to heal. To discover when and where the initial offense took place, and why you may have harbored the pain and feelings, and how to move forward - "bob and weave". Timing is important. A boxer doesn't bob and weave while leaving himself unguarded. Bobbing and weaving is a calculated technique against an attack. Whether you're moving defensively or offensively – arm yourself against emotional attacks with prayer. Pray for yourself, your corner man, and your opponent.

Jump Ship?!

Some people take 'jump ship' to mean 'get out of here' and find a way to get out as quickly as possible or by any means necessary. It's often an approach taken when challenging situations occur in life. Are you ready to get out of situations before you learn the lesson and gain insight, or ensure a safe departure? When you debark hastily without consideration for how and where you're headed, and whether you have the proper or appropriate equipment to get you there, you may approach the next situation ill-prepared. Understand what it takes to be successful where you are and where you're going; and plan an exit strategy in the beginning. One of the first things passengers do after boarding a cruise ship and before leaving the dock is to practice an emergency evacuation drill. Don't jump ship: learn how to exit gracefully and strategically.

Replay

Have you ever wondered why we move forward in time, rather than backwards or in repetition? In life, we experience a lot of good moments we wish we could replay and even relive, but only briefly ponder those moments occasionally; while some of the bad moments, we can't seem to get beyond. Why is it that most of our emotions are tied to the things we had less control over? How do we use/replay the good memories to get us through time and to overcompensate for the bad? I believe our focus should be on creating and experiencing more great moments in life, to create even better memories.

Trust in God's deliverance and faithfulness.

In the Meantime

He's all you need in the middle of your situation. Trust that what's next is already what's happening now. Believe that what you're seeking to obtain, you've already attained by accepting the vision, plotting the course and experiencing the plan. "Getting ready" started at (I do/I will/I have accepted) the thought of anticipating your next move. The meantime is intended to take place, to manifest the expected – live as if what you believe has already been revealed.

Got Armor?

Protect yourself against fear in the same manner that you would protect against danger. Fear is crippling and can cause you to lose sight of your purpose. It can also lead to a lack of self-confidence, self-esteem and faith. When you continually think you can't complete your project because you lack the proper tools, it's as though you wonder whether you should've even started. In some cases, there's a process of elimination: to discover what needs to be done now, later or never. But when it's a task that needs to be done, and only the fear of doing it or the fear of how to complete the task is standing in your way, then stand up to the fear. Inquire of others who have excelled in the path you're embarking upon; and you will discover the task at hand is doable because you have the tools (armor) to be successful. Identify and arm yourself with the necessary tools to accomplish your feat.

You're often chosen for your assignment before bearing

the armor to go into battle.

(Inspired by 1 Samuel 16-17, MSG)

Growth

Everyone grows at various rates and in different seasons. An individual's season of growth is unique to their journey to destiny. Realize that through each growth spurt victory is experienced. Celebrate every step toward your (and other's) growth to success!

How Do You Handle the Pause?

Normally when you press the pause button on the remote to briefly interrupt a movie, it's because you need to do something productive that just can't wait until the end.

Well, what do you do if you feel that someone has pressed the pause button on your life? And it would have to be someone other than yourself because if truth be told you surely wouldn't have pressed pause now, not when knowing what's next to come seems critical for you to do today, at the very least to prepare for it. And you don't even know how to prepare for it because you don't know what you're preparing for: just keep being productive anyway on what you think you should be doing.

Besides, the only One who knows what's next has also pressed the mute button or so it seems. So, I might as well read the Word (captions). At least when reading the summary of a movie it gives you an idea of how the movie will end. Well, so will reading the Word (Bible), every part unfolds the promises for your life. Enjoy the pause in life to live fully in God's promise.

Champagne Life

In this season, campaign on behalf of important issues and understand what is important to you. Know that the decision you make today also affects someone else's tomorrow.

The right to vote and the right to any decision is a privilege provided to us because of the decisions made by our ancestors. Let your decisions positively impact the generations to follow.

"Champaign Life": Celebrate the best life afforded us by God's grace and mercy!

"(God) Your grace and mercy brought me through. I'm living this moment because of You."

(Inspired by 'Your Grace and Mercy' by Mississippi Mass Choir)

ROI

Find ways to give back with no immediate ROI (return on investment). Your collected and shared treasures, both mental/emotional and physical, will be an asset as you seek to advance in life.

If you have ever had a job, then you have participated in the business. You have invested your time, skills and services to the success of the organization. At the time of employment, were your thoughts filled with gratitude or disgrace? Did you step up to lead or settle for the bare minimum? When you do not give or attempt to give 100% of your best every day, then it is as though at the end of the pay period your payment is zero.

If you were ever dependent upon a single leader keeping the organization in operation, then now is the time to refocus, partner with other leaders and exceed expectations in all you do, which yields a higher return of investment.

Thru the Tunnel

It's so dark I could close my eyes and wouldn't know the difference. Oh my, what did I just trip over? And what is that smell? It doesn't smell like roses. If I don't get through this soon, I don't think I'm going to make it.

If you've ever gone through a dark tunnel, you know it feels like you'll never see light again. And while it may seem as though all your other senses are heightened (sense of smell, hearing and touch), you wonder if you'll ever recover. You'll go through tunnels in life as you move from one point to the next on the way to your destination. Darkness may overpower you; but it's only temporary. As long as you keep moving towards the light and staying on the straight path, the light in you will flicker until it becomes brighter than the darkness that surrounds you. When you get through the tunnel and breathe a sigh of relief, you'll see more clearly, listen more attentively and be more aware of your surroundings. Go thru the tunnel. Don't let it overtake you.

I Deserve It

Show God you deserve to be blessed. Although His plan doesn't quite match up with what you would like to have now, understand that He knows your past, present and your days to come. What you desired to have so badly, He's not removing from you as a punishment - He's delivering to you a better lifestyle.

Look Like Where You're Headed

We've all heard the saying that it's best to look like where you're headed than where you've been. Or some like to say, 'dress the part'. There is wisdom in this saying. The way that we present ourselves often opens the doors to the new opportunities that we desire.

On the hurried days when you may feel you barely have enough time to carry out the activities of life, just try to slow down and recall what's most important. Focus on these things and the peace you hope for will come.

How Much Do You Love Yourself?

I was challenged by the commandment, *"love your neighbor as yourself" (Leviticus 19:18, MSG),* because for a second I was living "love your neighbor, or do for your neighbor, more than yourself." It was as if it was a generational curse for me: I had seen relatives live in this manner and haphazardly followed suit. But you'll know when a particular lifestyle, borne of good intentions or not, just doesn't fit. You'll become more aggravated with life and feel as though nothing is going right.

So how do you faithfully live by the commandment without being selfish? Often extreme measures are taken when we make a change from one behavior or action to another. Therefore, it's best to gradually achieve a healthy, stable state.

A healthy "yes" to self could also benefit others and this decision will help you live a joyous life.

Monique K. Turrentine

Chapter 6
Love

Monique K. Turrentine

A Compassionate Heart

Have you ever thought of living life as someone else? What if you experienced the life of someone less fortunate? A person's life is not only predicated on the choices they make but also the opportunities they are provided.

Pay attention to the choices you make. Continue to give others a chance at success. Hold the door open for others to follow.

Love Me

How do you love? There's not an answer that I'm seeking; it's a question for self-discovery. How do you love or show love to others? Most importantly, how do you love yourself? Not in a narcissistic manner, but in the fashion of showing reverence and honor to God, your Creator. Love yourself as though your joy, peace and strength are dependent upon it.

This Must Be Love

With just one touch, you felt your strength renewed.

With just one word, you could sense the familiarity in the unfamiliar.

With just one breath, your life is resuscitated.

This is Love.

What Do You Want to Get in This Life?

Have you ever wanted something so desperately that you saved every dollar until you got it? Well, that's the way we should feel about living life fully each day. We should be desperate to live a life full of love, faith and compassion. Life is valuable. Jesus lived each day desperate to heal, love and teach (about righteousness). Some people may feel that the situations in His day were different from what we experience today, but I believe the times are similar; all people then and now need to be loved and healed. Give love to get more out of life.

Love Anyhow

Just as there are questions, there are also answers. Oftentimes though, we feel as if we have more questions than answers. One question that often challenges many people even in various situations is, "How do I love in and through this?" But there is an answer: "Love anyhow." Even in difficult incidents, love has a way of freeing and healing. Love is the answer in all situations.

We love because He first loved us. (1 John 4, MSG)

Freely

I've heard people say that nothing is free. So, what about love? What price did you pay for love? Some people put a dollar sign on sacrifice, and say they've sacrificed for love. But I've never seen it (sacrifice) weighed. Until I learned that sacrifice was only weighed and counted once, and it was a balanced weight (*on the cross*).

The One who gave His life on the cross was also the One who received our life. His life for ours, and we are all His - we all balance the weight when we believe in Him. So then, love was freely given to us, we didn't pay for it. Therefore, we must freely give love.

An Excerpt from a Love Letter

"God has smiled on me, He has set me free...God has smiled on me, He's been good to me."

Lord, when I think of your love towards me, I am filled with joy. Your intricate care and protection for me is amazing. You know my needs and exceed my expectations: You are Jehovah Jireh (my provider)! Every moment I learn a new aspect of You; and seek to know and love You even more, even to mimic your everlasting love to others.

Relationships are an interesting part of life. A combination of love and pain, faith and reality, and confidence and inabilities. You can be in a relationship and still feel alone; or be single with great friends and still not find it easier to go through the relationship. In either scenario, pain and heartache aren't so easy to escape. When you've said and heard enough, you don't even want to process the options.

People often say all pain is the same, whether external or internal; it's the decisions you face that are similar. You may feel like it's your last moment, like any second you could flip, but you've made up in your mind to live this way - keep trusting. Yes, trust in God, the One who has seen you through this moment, who has fixed the pain, who has healed your heart. He has all control, all power.

Stay focused on His will and His Word. That's your way of escape, true freedom, and soon you'll feel better. This moment will be a memory and laughter will fill your heart and joy resonate through your life. You'll win in this. You'll survive even this. Keep thinking good thoughts and maintain a grateful attitude.

(Inspired by 'God Has Smiled on Me' by Rev. James Cleveland)

Chapter 7
Relationships

Monique K. Turrentine

Relationships

What is a real relationship? How do we really show love? What does love look like? Is the love we show to others as transparent as Jesus' sacrificial death on the cross? Or as open as God's arms even before we confess our sins? Perhaps love looks to us like "tough love," expecting from someone else what we cannot deliver to others.

A real relationship is established from love. It is a partnership, a brother-/sisterhood, to love your brother/sister and want the best for them despite their (and your) flaws. God's love, showcased through Jesus' death, burial and resurrection, is reenacted best when we accept our flaws as humans, cast aside the past pains, forgive, and love more, again.

When Jesus was resurrected, He did not look the same way He did on the cross. There was a newness, which was only apparent after some time. His process took three days. However, God's grace and mercy towards us is new every morning. Our love for one another should be the same.

Transparency

How do you become transparent with people you don't know? How do you balance sharing your testimony without the fear of ridicule, judgment or abandonment? How is it that death is more painful than resurrection? Sometimes sharing our testimonies can feel like we are reliving the 'death' of our past situation; however, we are actually helping to give birth to new life.

You are unique when you allow others to know more about you; when it goes beyond seeing how you work to seeing why you live. Transparency comes with discernment. Guard your heart in the things you say and do with others. Be willing to share your testimony when pertinent. All things operate in divine timing.

Your Breakthrough Connector

Have you ever tried to get power to a lamp without plugging it in? What about electricity from a socket without the proper adapter? Getting a powerful breakthrough is like an electric circuit; one has to serve the purpose for the other and they must be connected to get the power source. Our prayers are connectors. When we unite/link with another person in prayer, we're able to hear God more clearly, surrender to His will and commit all our weakness to get His strength. You know you're connected to the right person when you feel the power of God working through the both of you.

Imagine how powerful our prayers would be if we're linked with *several* people – just think of a surge protector and how much power is generated to multiple devices.

Beyond Myself

Get me beyond myself so that I can be more concerned for others. Get me beyond myself so I can love more, care more and pray more; so the trials of life no longer take over people's lives. Teach me how to be a witness, how to be an encourager, and a soldier for Christ.

Measure it First

Things can always look better when it's measured against its own kind. But what about when you measure it up to what it's supposed to be. You don't quite count the flaws; rather the things that are right. Measure it first to what it should be, then you'll see that it fits.

(Inspired by Colossians 3, MSG)

A Good Connection

In the age of social media of connecting with everyone (family, friends, coworkers, and even strangers), it's easy to mistake "tagging" a friend or sending a "tweet" for an actual connection. Cherish the moments you can spend genuinely connecting in person with a family member or friend. It's good to take advantage of the various ways to contact people through social media, but there's never a replacement to the quality time you spend with people.

Friend'ar

Do you have a friend radar - a gauge that tells you the type of friend you are? There are times when we have people/friends in our life to warn us against ourselves; to let us know that we aren't being a good friend. Those types of friends are in our lives for a season. Check your "friend'ar". While some friendship ties need to be severed, others need to be nurtured. Know the difference between closure and clarification. In certain situations, both need mutual agreement and understanding before moving forward. Learn to be friendlier to all friends. Godly friendships are important to your well-being.

"Our Inheritance is Freedom"

Liberation is often a loosely used word by people still in bondage, whether bound by a type of employment, ideology, or system. Once you've reached your level of freedom, what does or should it look like? Doesn't freedom still imply some level of serving or being used? Or better yet, can a servant truly be free? Can a worker be liberated? Yes! It depends on who you work for and who or what you believe in. True freedom rests in the Beholder, the one who alleviates all burdens/stress and frees you to serve in your true calling so that it doesn't feel like bondage. Forgiveness is freeing. If we are to cast all our cares to the one who cares for us, then we should truly live freely to be effective members (in a bound society) to help lead others to freedom.

Gather Together

I was reading a book and came across a profound statement:

People have a responsibility to one another and that's to treat each other well.

I thought about how different we all are and how differences have become our frailties rather than our strengths. We are better as a group of people because we are different. Like the parts of our body - our eyes are different from our head, ears, fingers, arms, legs, heart, lungs, brain, and so on. But each part serves a purpose for the entire body. We should seek to understand, care for and respect one another. We are all here to live together in unity and fulfill our purpose together.

Tradition

Tradition can become ineffective repetition when there is no historical relevance. Cultural traditions can be successful legacies when properly transmitted. As discovered in the book 'Outliers' by Malcolm Gladwell, an entire community of Rosetans lived healthy and successful lives because of the traditions they valued from their history in Italy. Knowledge of your family's legacy can help you live a healthy lifestyle.

Monique K. Turrentine

This is Our Block

When you feel like you've lost something valuable, that's when you're ready to claim everything you own. Even the things you once gave away, you're eager to retrieve. But can you truly count everything you have? Are you able to share your most valuable possession? Well, this is what happens when you lose it or even give it away - you're sharing it. When people are lost, that's God's way of sharing His most valuable possession with us. We're to care for, love and support those who have lost their way and guide them back to their rightful Owner. On our block, we care for all of our own.

Hold on Tight

Who's got a hold on you? A hold so tight that their control of your decision makes it almost impossible for you to think for yourself. So why give someone that much power over your life? Has your concern for impressing others gone beyond the care you take for yourself? Do you even recognize their grasp? Do you gasp for air at their grasp? Hold tighter to what you know and believe. Hold on tight to your own plans and goals so that others have no hold on you.

Think About It

When we've encountered an interesting situation, like an unexpected occurrence we barely had expectations for – we're taken off-guard. We put too much thought into a thoughtless act, either on our part or the other person's actions (or lack thereof). Let's say for instance, there's a miscommunication and you're left thinking, "what went wrong?" Your thoughts replay the conversation (highlighting your side, of course) and you think about it until you run out of possible scenarios and 'what ifs'. Allowing your mind to overthink a situation is unhealthy. Either settle in your heart that you'll have a conversation about it, forgive and forget about it, or think about how you'll move forward.

Don't Ask

When you don't ask, you don't get the answer you're looking for. But what about when the answer seems apparent, yet you still don't ask? What if the person genuinely cares and just wants to ask, "how are you?" – only to be interrupted with "don't ask". When we shut people out or fail to continue learning, we're closing off the possibility of discovery. The next time you're tempted to not inquire or to be discovered – think about what you and others can gain in the process of asking.

Monique K. Turrentine

Who Am I To You, Now?

Now that you're older and have had more experiences, gone through some trials and excelled in your goals, who am I to you? Am I still the one you seek for insight or to share your deepest secrets and desires? Do you question whether I can deliver in the things you overlooked before? Maybe I didn't handle you with care and lost my temper when you needed me there. So, who am I to you now? Do you think my love for you has changed, or can I measure up to your expectations? I may not have said or properly expressed it before, but I know who I am now. I am who God called me to be. I am at my best, to you now, is who I am.

Unproductive Dialogue

It's time to spend less time letting your thoughts run rampant on worthless items. What you think is often reflected in your speech. In order to transform into productive dialogue, focus your mind on more positive topics.

Getting it Right

Relationships can be difficult to navigate, especially covenant relationships when day-to-day tasks have the tendency to loosen the bond.

What's in it for me?

I think there are times when we are consumed with saying what needs to be said at an inopportune time, that we focus on the delivery and miss the content. All messages are meant to be heard but not commanded. When messages are spoken in love, what is said is often better received. Learn your loved ones' love language.

So, we think we've covered the 'love' subject until we are on the defense; but we are only reaping what we have sown/previously spoken. My recommendation is to "get it right"! When you feel like you are talking to your spouse or loved one harshly, tune up and imagine you are talking to Jesus because you are, in essence, talking to Him.

The Original

Marriage is like a building, which makes the foundation vital. If the structure is destroyed by sin, or conditional love, and the Architect has been fired, then you have the opportunity to rebuild the structure on a solid foundation. Think of when you have seen a brick building demolished: it is rare that the structure is rebuilt exactly as the original. However, when buildings maintain their initial solid foundation; they withstand catastrophes. It is important to maintain the foundation of your marriage and core of your being, which is your heart. To prevent a destroyed structure: keep God first, pray for strength in all things, and love unconditionally (the agape way of love).

> *"Therefore everyone who hears these words of mine and puts them into practice is like a wise man who built his house on the rock. The rain came down, the streams rose, and the winds blew and beat against that house; yet it did not fall, because it had its foundation on the rock." (Matthew 7:24-25, NIV)*

The Covenant

I don't have a problem with my marriage. We talk about everything. He knows my every move and I let Him check my phone.

I don't have a problem with my marriage. He makes me laugh, and wipes my tears when I cry. He comforts me and gives me strength.

I don't have a problem with my marriage. We don't argue or fuss, but He lets me vent and takes time to help me sort through my issues. I trust Him, and confide in Him.

I don't have a problem with my marriage. He pays for the things I want and need, and treats me like a queen. He says kind things and gives me everything, and I serve Him only.

You see, I don't have a problem with my marriage because He loves me unconditionally, teaches me how to worship and praise. We sing and rejoice even in seemingly bad days.

I don't have a problem with my marriage. I don't raise my voice or take out my frustrations on Him. Though my love for Him will never measure up to His love for me, His sacrifice and victories.

Isn't this what marriage is supposed to be?

Chapter 8
Follow the Leader

Monique K. Turrentine

Follow the Leader

Focus on leadership and know that God has called you to be the leader of your purpose. Become an effective leader by being aware of the needs of others and having compassion for others. Consistently have your mind and heart filled with ways to bless people. (Inspired by Galatians 6:10, MSG)

The life of a leader is always examined by people. It is important that your light shines bright and you continue to sharpen your skills. "Let your light shine to men to be a witness of God's glory."

Recognize

I don't recognize it anymore: the ebbs and flows, variables and inconsistencies cause doubt and I lose sight of the context.

"What did he say?"

"I did what?"

The conversation is unclear and sight still blurred. I can't even see what it says, do I even understand?

"Am I losing the connection?"

I must have missed the transition. How did I get here and not recognize or realize it? Wasn't He supposed to tell me when I started slippin', I mean 'slipping'. Even the language of the world has overtaken me – wisdom is no longer valued. Where did I go astray? When did I think I was right without any regard to His insight? I was busy seeking symbols and shortcuts, that meanings are no longer important. How did I not recognize I arrived at this convoluted state?

Out of Order

In how many ways does He need to get your attention? He orchestrates interruptions in normal routines to get a message to you; to catch you when you're present and listening. He breaks the formation to ensure you recognize His presence. When things in life don't appear to be working properly; God will disrupt your plan to let you know He's got you aligned with His will.

"I Do"

If I could ever express Your love, I know it wouldn't be enough to exact upon the many ways You've blessed me. If I could ever feel Your embrace (gasp), a breath through which You speak, I couldn't imagine the response. Just how much You love, I know – just how much You give, I feel – just how grand You are, I love. If I could see Your face, my love, I'd know I couldn't explain the beauty of Your embrace. For words could not explain Your voice which is calming as dew; to focus on Your command – "I Do". I love to see Your hand at work – Your mighty works come through. I follow Your guide as You see us through; You pinpoint our steps in You and count our flawless ways. Through Your blood I see the floodgates of love. You know my heart, my everlasting love.

Know Your Role

When you get a new job or opportunity, you do not know your role and responsibility until you are in the position and doing what is expected of you. You may have an idea of what is expected but until you are working, the tasks are unclear.

How do you learn in your new role? What steps do you take to find out what to do? How do you fit in the culture of the organization? Ask questions, read a lot, practice, learn from the One who knows it all and make adjustments. You will excel!

King Me

In the game of checkers, the purpose is to be king. Actually, this is God's purpose for us as well, to become king *(not gender specific)*. He told Adam and Eve to have dominion on earth. With God as our Lord, we can lead effectively.

To live a kingdom lifestyle, you must know what you value, your non-negotiable(s) and your next move.

When playing checkers, there are individual pieces. The significance of the term "king me" signifies two pieces coming together. The importance of a king's/leader's role is to unite. Are you uniting with other believers, your spouse, your family, your friends?

Although Adam and Eve selfishly decided to take the fall, they stood together when they took responsibility for their actions and answered to God. Imagine our power as united believers and leaders taking authority in obedience to His call on our lives. Join the KING!

Move Closer

Take a step closer in order to receive the reward, win the game and accept the honor of being king. Each step closer to the KING is vital to your success.

> *"Come close to God [with a contrite heart] and He will come close to you." (James 4:8, AMP)*

Perfected

Our Perfect Creator made everything perfect. He never makes mistakes. Therefore, we are perfect, but only in Him. So, when we make mistakes, accept it and correct it, and align to His Perfect will.

A-Line

When preparing for a performance or an important meeting, we practice or work until its right. Then it's time for the performance or presentation.

Our presentation of ourselves is often our outward appearance. Look at your outfit, is it wrinkled? Well, iron it, straighten it. Sometimes straightening a wrinkle is all the change needed. *Physical wrinkles come with age, but spiritual ones shouldn't.* Being bent out of shape or combating issues that come along the way just need a little aligning: prepare through prayer.

"A-line" (align) to His will and that will perfect you.

Being perfected is to be the best you can be!

Try Harder

Giving up too soon never measured up to much. The process of starting again can seem overwhelming. So, what do you do when you want to give up? Try Harder! Get a different perspective of what you're dealing with, talk and work through your challenges, and then realize that you're not in it alone. There's always a greater Guide (God) to help you excel.

Return to Sender

Have you ever routinely opened an envelope only to realize the letter isn't addressed to you? What about getting an invitation back, stamped with "Return to Sender" when only part of the address was misconstrued? Well, I wonder what it's like when God is watching us on the hurried path of life; only for us to discover we've detoured a few years askew from our destined route. Sometimes, we're so off-center that we can't easily quite interpret our misstep. We go through the process of elimination and redirection to identify which is the correct path. But once the letter is returned to the sender, similar to when we return to our Sender, it/we will be sure to arrive at the originally intended destination.

Addicted to Dreams

Do you often catch yourself in a long stare, or has anyone interrupted a lucid thought? You may be addicted to dreams! What are dreams really about? At some point do the 'good' ones come true, or the seemingly 'real' ones take effect? There's minimal reality in a full dream; you may experience parts of it when awake, but dreams are often restful or restless places. When you find it's easier to accept a dream, then wake up to reality because dreaming is never enough. Let God reveal to you all that He has in store for you. Take the limits off God, and feel free to dream in His reality.

Seek Him

Seek the Lord, while He may be found.

"Wake me up, Dear God, wake me up! I do not want to miss the moment of your speech, or have my lamp snuffed out preventing me from moving when you call. Wake me up, God; I know I cannot be there yet. I know that there is more for me."

I had an issue of loving rest. It was something about the serenity of being asleep that kept me in bed too long. Though some restful nights were not peaceful, they were better than facing an ill-perceived, unsuccessful day. I felt like I was in the film 'Avatar', awake while asleep. Studies have shown that enough sleep is healthy but too much sleep is unhealthy. Get up when it is time and be thankful to face a new day!

Monique K. Turrentine

A Message from God

What are you concerned about? Don't you know I got you? I have this situation, just like I had the other situations – even though you thought you had it covered. Even when you didn't ask Me about it. I just knew you would come to Me at some point, but you tried to handle it all yourself. And how did that go? And now that it's come to this – are you tired yet? Are you overworked? Do you realize that you weren't given this task because of your capability but because of your inability? Because I knew that you would have to depend on Me through this task from beginning to end. Yes, it's about Me – in case you forgot why you're here and why you're faced with making this decision again. But I got you now just like I had you then. Come to Me, and give your all to Me. I'm not going to leave you or forsake you.

With Love, Your Almighty God

(Inspired by Isaiah 43:1-3, MSG)

130

IMAGE CONFIDENCE ESTEEM

Monique K. Turrentine

About the Author

Monique K. Turrentine is a native of North Carolina with a passion for helping others in their personal development and enhancing their image. She founded Image Confidence Esteem while earning a Bachelor of Arts degree in English at UNC Chapel Hill. Monique has also attained a master's degree and a successful career in Human Resources. While pursuing a career in Human

Resources, she concurrently became a licensed Cosmetologist and has offered services ranging from presenting unique designs for fashion and hair shows to providing one-on-one consultations and personal styling sessions. In 2010, she launched a quarterly newsletter to empower and enlighten individuals, which marked the beginning of her personal writing and motivational speaking venture. Monique continues to engage and inspire audiences and readers as they proceed through the journey of life.

Made in the USA
Columbia, SC
25 May 2023